GLIMPSES OF
COTTERED

Highlights of the villages of
Cottered, Throcking and Broadfield
over the centuries

by
Neville Chuck

Front cover: *Cottered from the south 1994*

Title page: *Centre of Cottered 1960's*

Published by The Friends of Cottered Church.

Copyright © The Friends of Cottered Church. 2006
ISBN 10: 0-9553142-0-8
ISBN 13: 978-0-9553142-0-9
Printed in England by
Streets Printers, Royston Road, Baldock, Herts. SG7 6NW

Contents

Acknowledgements

The Author would like to thank the following people who all contributed in some way.

Ann Aldridge, Ivy Anderson, Bert and Joyce Cartwright, Derek Charles, Carol Clark, Sam Cooper, Fred Dowton, Wilf Dowton, Dick Edwards, Shirley Fowler, Jo Hayden, Ann King, Mary King, Percy Kingsley, Sally Kingsley, Eileen Knight, Joan and Mary Knight, Rose McKay, Ivy and Ted Newman, Frank Pinnock, Dorothy Reed, Peter Sanders, Duncan Saunders, Melanie Shaw, Audrey and Vic Silsby, Pep Skipp, Vera Slazak, Jessie and Phil Vine, Molly and Stan Wilds and Shirley Wilson.

The author also acknowledges the help of the East Hertfordshire Archaeological Society, Hertfordshire Archives and Local Studies, the Cottered and Throcking News, the Churchwardens of Cottered and Throcking and the Royston Crow.

Bibliography
Bussby, F. *Winchester Cathedral 1079-1979*
Chauncy, H. *Historical Antiquities of Hertfordshire*
Clutterbuck, R. *History of Hertfordshire*
Cockman, G. C. *Discovering Lost Railways*
Curtis, G. *A Chronicle of Small Beer*
East Herts. *Archaeological Society Transactions*
Gover, J. E. B., Mawer, A. & Stenton, F. M. *The Place-Names of Hertfordshire*
Hurt, J. S. *Bringing Literacy to Rural England*
Kelly's Directories
Kinross, J. *Discovering Castles in England and Wales*
Klingelhofer, E. *The Deserted Medieval Village of Broadfield*
Kusumoto, S. *Cottered: the Japanese Garden*
Mange, F. *Portrait of a Decade: the 1940's*
Markwell, F. C. & Saul, P. *Tracing your Ancestors the A-Z Guide*
Pitkin Guides The Normans
Richardson, J. *The Local Historian's Encyclopaedia*
Salmon, N. *History of Hertfordshire*
Stratton, B. (Ed.) *Cottered through the Centuries*
Urwick, W. *Non-conformity in Hertfordshire.*
Victoria County History of Hertfordshire

All photographs are by the author except where stated otherwise.
Sadly, there was not space to include all the pictures chosen for this book.

Every effort has been made to ensure the information in this book is accurate and the author regrets any errors or omission that may have occurred.

Foreword

THE BISHOP OF ST ALBANS
The Rt Revd Christopher Herbert

It is a privilege to have been asked to write the Foreword to this book. I was very willing to accept Neville Chuck's kind challenge to do so, partly because of my own love of local history but also because I wanted to use it as a way of offering my own thanks to Neville for his tireless and faithful service as organist, choirmaster and churchwarden at Cottered over many years. That kind of steadfast commitment is in increasingly short supply - but it is part of what makes life in rural England very special.

One of the tests of writing about local history is whether it leaves the reader wanting to know more. This book passes that test with flying colours. When I read it, I wanted to know more about Widow Herbert (not surprisingly), more about the field names - who or what was Trigwells? I wanted to know more about the Bumpy Tree, more about the Revd Angel Chauncy and the Revd Anthony Trollope, more about the old church at Broadfield, more about the blacksmiths and brewers and shoemakers - in fact, more about much more. No doubt other people will ask other questions. But then, that is what local history does; it catches the imagination and challenges us to think about the way we have gained so much from the lives of those who have gone before us.

The other test of local history writing is whether or not it catches what can only be described as a 'sense of place'. Again, this book does that and through its careful choice of subjects and people, ensures that the uniqueness of Cottered as a community is revealed.

It is written with enjoyment, wit and a feel for the wryness of things but, perhaps above all, it illuminates not only the transience of life but also those underlying qualities of permanence which make life worthwhile and full of meaning.

You may have guessed that I enjoyed reading this book enormously; I hope that it will stimulate other histories in other villages. For those who come after us it will be, as the author says, a glimpse of life in the twentieth and twenty-first centuries in this particular corner of Hertfordshire. It is a quiet and delightful treasure.

+ Christopher St Albans

Author's Note

T he idea for this book arose from two "Our Village" talks organized by the Friends of Cottered Church, who raise much needed funds for church repairs. The Friends agreed to back the project financially, with profits going towards the organisation's funds.

For several decades I was the village correspondent for some of the local newspapers and worked for the Royston Crow, first as a reporter and then as a photographer. I am indeed grateful to the Crow's current Editor, Les Baker, who has given his permission for numerous articles and photos to be used in this book. I have also drawn heavily on local County histories, the Hertfordshire Archives and Local Studies (HALS) and visited some older villagers, many whom have since passed away.

My sincere thanks to the Right Reverend Christopher Herbert, the Bishop of St. Albans, for the foreword, to Esther Taylor for her extensive work in editing and to all those people have given their support and encouragement in this two year project. Particular thanks are due to Gail Hickman, Dr. Barry Price, Erika Williams, Bill Johnston and Steve Auckland for their proof reading and helpful suggestions.

Neville Chuck
June 2006

Neville Chuck 1966

Early Days

The civil parish of Cottered, some 3,254 acres, incorporates Broadfield and Throcking, once parishes in their own right. The villages are situated between two Roman Roads, Ermine Street, the present A10, to the east and Stane Street to the west. The area is fertile with easy access to a water supply and numerous springs. The old River Bourne to the east and the River Beane to the west both have sources in the parish. Thistley Vale Brook, which runs into the Rib at Buntingford, begins at Throcking.

Long before the Romans came, Bronze Age peoples lived in the area to the north. Fragments of a dagger and a portion of a sword from the Bronze Age were discovered at Cumberlow Green, just over the Cottered boundary. Stane Street, a Roman road leading from Colchester via Braughing to Baldock and then on to Godmanchester, is known locally as Back Lane. Now only a grassy lane, its imposing width can give a glimpse of how it once was. William Stukeley (1687 - 1765), who began a fashionable interest in antiquities, mentions a discovery of coins in a barrow near Cottered, dating from the Roman-British period.

Roman Road, Stane Street, on the boundary between Cottered and Ardeley 1999

It is thought there were Saxon settlements here, but the first documented reference to the three parishes is in the Domesday Book, published in 1087.

Much of the parish stands on high ground at just below 500 ft above sea level. It is claimed that the next highest ground to the east are the Ural Mountains! Where the parishes of Cottered, Throcking and Broadfield all meet at Foxholes, the longitude is 0.03' 58" west of the Greenwich Meridian line and 51' 57" latitude, putting it in line with Calgary, Warsaw and the Aleutian Islands.

Each parish has its own church, apart from Broadfield, whose church was destroyed by fire in the mid 15th century. Cottered was once divided into two manors; the Manor of Cottered, also known as The Lordship, and Cheynes Manor, while Broadfield and Throcking both had their own manors. Broadfield manor house has been rebuilt several times while that of Throcking was demolished in 1744 following a family dispute. The Lordship at Cottered dates from the 14th century, but the location of Cheynes Manor house is not known for certain.

When William the Conqueror became king, he gave Cottered, or Chodrei as it was then known, to one of his relations, Walkelin, who was Bishop of Winchester. Bishop Walkelin was a somewhat devious character. He asked the King for timber for the new cathedral he was building. King William told him he could have as much as he could gather from the royal wood nearby in four days and nights. Only one tree was left in the wood when the Bishop's men finished the job!

Over the centuries, the names of all three villages have evolved to their present forms. Experts do not all agree on the meanings of the names, but some think that Cottered denotes a 'cold ridge', while others suggest 'a stream where the fish spawn'. The 'ing' in Throcking implies that the name is Saxon. The Old English 'throcc' was the name for part of a wooden ploughshare. Broadfield appears to be the obvious 'broad field', a wide open space, or possibly 'broad fell', a hill.

MAP   3

Cottered

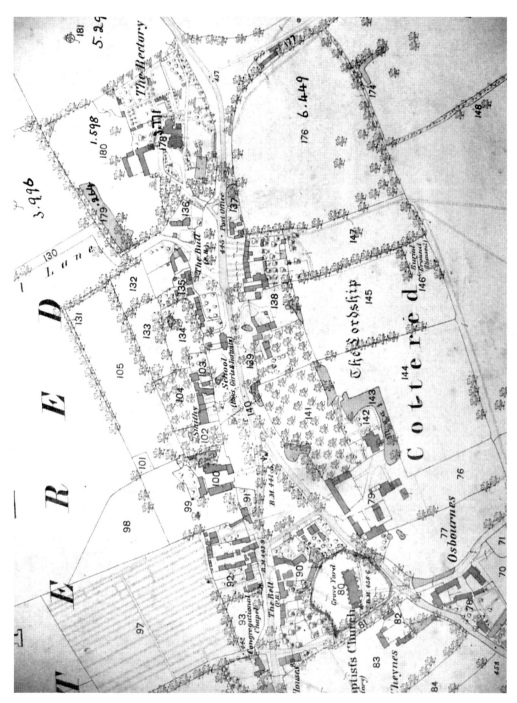

Map by Ordnance Survey 1876

The Manors of Cottered

Cottered was divided into two manors, Cheynes Cottered and Cottered Lordship. Each manorial holding had its own Court which enforced local customs and regulations. Decisions were taken by twelve jurors, known as the Homage, and the rulings were recorded on a Court Roll.

Not all the Court Rolls for Cottered have survived the passage of time, but those that have are held in the County Record Office in Hertford.

When property and lands changed hands, either when the owner died or when they were 'alienated', or sold, each incoming tenant had to make a payment to the lord and swear an oath of allegiance known as 'fealty'. Tenants would be given a copy of the transaction as their title deed. By carefully following the descent or sale of these properties, it has been possible in some cases to find out the owners through the centuries down to the 1820's.

Each time the Court was held there is a list of jurors who sat and those who sent their apologies for non-attendance, for which there was a fine. The Court elected a Constable who had many duties; the upkeep of the stocks, apprenticing pauper children, collecting rates and convening the parish meeting, to mention but a few. They also elected a Pinder, who was responsible for stray cattle and putting them in a pound until they were claimed.

During the early part of the 12th century, Cheynes Manor was formed out of Cottered Manor. It became known as Cheyney-Cottered or Cheines Place. For a period King Henry III, who reigned for 56 years, held it. In 1248 he granted all William de Ken's lands, which included Cottered, to William Chesney. The name Cheynes was taken from the family who held it at this period.

The manor passed through the Chesney family and on to Anne, who married Sir John Willoughby. They had one son, Robert. A staunch supporter of King Henry VII, Sir Robert played a prominent part in the Wars of the Roses, fighting in the Battle of Bosworth Field in 1485. He was created Lord Willoughby de Broke as a reward.

Emma Lacey on the doorstep at The Place, Flanders Green 1920's,
believed to be the site of the old Cheines Place.
Picture loaned by Steve Auckland

Cheynes descended eventually to Sir Foulk Greville, who was created Baron Brooke in January 1621. But in 1628 a servant, who considered that his services had been insufficiently rewarded, stabbed him. Another Lord of this Manor was George Verney, Baron Willougby de Broke, Dean of Windsor. The estate descended with the Willoughby de Brokes until it was sold in the 1820s to the Newbold family who held it until it they sold the land to Herbert Goode at the beginning of the 20th century.

The surviving manor house known as The Lordship was built about 1428 by Sir John Fray, Chief Baron of the Exchequer. The property still retains a large proportion of the original moat. Edward Pulter acquired the estate in the 16th century, along with that of Broadfield, and the two manors descended together until the early 20th century.

The moated site which may have been where an early manor house once stood next to Brixbury, the present playing field 2006.

There are several homestead moats in the area, such as the one next to Brixbury, the playing field in Cottered. There is a similar one, called The Island, east of Flanders Green. At Throcking there is one north of the Old Rectory and another where Throcking Manor House once stood.

The Court Rolls for Cottered Lordship date from 1633. In 1659, the Court ordered that all the occupiers of the farm called the Lordship should keep 360 sheep; John Wallis 100, William Bennett 120, Thomas Dunn for part of Cheynes Farm 100 and Thomas Randall for part of Cheynes Farm 100.

In 1776 it was noted that, by ancient custom, the tenant of the Lordship ought to keep a bull and boar for the use of the tenants, they paying 4d (2p) for the bull and 2d (1p) for the boar 'as often as they shall have occasion to use them'. I expect this ensured they had good stock from which to breed.

The Lordship by J C Buckler 1832
HALS DE/Bg/2 p.147

Cheynes Farm 1900's
Photo loaned by Rose McKay

Broadfield

Map by Ordnance Survey 1876

The Manor of Broadfield

In the 12th century, one of the owners of the area known as Broadfield was Walter le Espec. He was a Justice of the Forest and an itinerant Justice in the North. At one time he held Warden Abbey in Bedfordshire and founded and endowed an abbey there. He resided at Helmsely Castle, Yorkshire. Espec founded both Kirkham Priory and Rievaulx Abbey, whose abbot Ailred describes him as a man of "immense height and build, with black hair, full beard, broad features and trumpet voice." Espec died in 1153.

The Black Death in 1349 is thought to be responsible for the disappearance of Broadfield.

Broadfield Church foundations uncovered during the dig 1965

A rescue dig was carried out by Philip Rahtz of the University of Birmingham over seven weeks in 1965. Three house plots were found; one may have been the manor house dating from before the church was built in about 1220. Fragments of the church and graves were discovered in the orchard of Hall Farm. The church itself was destroyed by fire in the mid 15th century.

Cottered artist Jo Hayden's impression of Broadfield Church

Broadfield estate survived and was owned in 1427 by Humphrey Stafford, first Duke of Buckingham, at the time the greatest land owner in England. The title remained in the Stafford family until the execution of Edward, the third Duke, in May 1521.

Broadfield Church looking east as uncovered in the dig 1965

Hall Farm 1987

Edward Pulter of Great Wymondley acquired the Broadfield estate in 1580 and around this time he also bought the Manor of Cottered.

Broadfield celebrated Queen Victoria's Diamond Jubilee in 1897 with a dinner in one of the barns on the estate. During the afternoon and evening there were games. A bonfire was lit on Hill Field and the day ended with a fireworks display.

More recent owners of Broadfield Hall include Prince Georg of Denmark and his wife, Princess Anne, a cousin of Queen Elizabeth II.

The Princes of Wales' aunt, the Hon Mary Gunningham and her husband Michael lived at Hall Farm for a time. They and their neighbour, Prince Georg of Denmark were both guests at the Royal Wedding of Prince Charles and Lady Diana Spencer.

Broadfield Hall by J. C. Buckler 1832
This mansion has been replaced, but the 17th century stable block remains
HALS DE/Bg/2 p.148

Her Highness Princess Anne
of Denmark 1972

His Highness Prince Georg
of Denmark 1982

Broadfield Hall 1959

Broadfield Hall 1920's
Photo loaned by Sally Kingsley

Once part of Broadfield Estate, Foxholes 2006

MAP   15

Throcking

Map by Ordnance Survey 1876

The Manor of Throcking

At the Domesday period, Throcking was owned jointly by Count Eustace of Boulogne, the Bishop of London, (probably Maurice), the Bishop of Bayeux, Odo, half brother to King William and Hardewin de Scalers.

Some centuries later, in 1549, a mansion at Throcking is mentioned. Among the lords of the Manor was Sir Leonard Hyde who, it is claimed, paved his kitchen at Hyde Hall, Sandon with gravestones from Throcking Church and embezzled the glebe. The manor passed to his son, who sold it in 1630 to Sir Thomas Soames, who in turn sold it to Councillor-at-law Robert Haworth of Gray's Inn during 1670. His daughter Frances married Jeremy Elwes.

The manor passed to Jeremy's eldest son, after whose death it came to his brother Robert, who in 1692 built a Manor House, Throcking Hall, on the meadow next to the churchyard at a cost of £10,000, only for it to be demolished 50 years later by his son Robert following a family dispute. Robert Elwes junior married Martha, the co-heiress of Richard Carey, one of the Governors of the Bank of England. Eventually the land was sold in parcels and the manorial rights lapsed.

The only building remaining from the 15th Century Throcking Hall, now converted to three dwellings 1995.

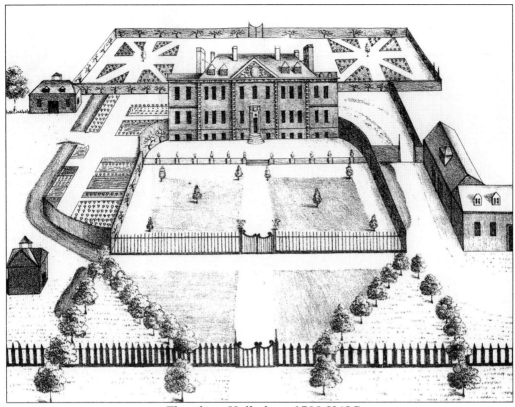

Throcking Hall about 1700 HALS
Chauncy's History Vol. 1

The Pightle on the site of the former mansion at Throcking 1962

Throcking Hall Farm 1930's
Photo loaned by Lavinia Baker

Council Houses and Throcking Water Tower 1993

By-Pass Built

T he first major road to be built at Throcking since the Romans constructed Ermine Street, the long awaited Buntingford By-Pass was opened ahead of schedule in June 1987.

The main trunk road from London, the A10, for centuries passed through the centre of Buntingford. A former toll gate on this stage coach route stood within Throcking parish.

The new by-pass, costing £3.4 million runs for almost half its length through the parish. The highway was opened by Local MP, Bowen Wells.

Bowen Wells, MP opens the Buntingford By-Pass watched by
Councillors Jane Pitman and Jon Ling 1987
Photo Royston Crow

Vow and Covenant

Du   uring the 1642 - 1649 Civil Wars between the Royalists
who supported King Charles and the Parliamentary Force
led by Oliver Cromwell, Cottered was on the side of
Parliament.

A copy of the "Vow & Covenant" dated June 1643 appears at the
rear of Cottered's oldest Parish Register. This was an agreement
made by members of the House of Commons to defend
Protestantism and the rights of Parliament, to which all males
over 18 years were expected to subscribe.

The Rector, the Rev Thomas Gardiner heads a list of no fewer
than 79 Cottered men.

The Church registers at Cottered date from 1558 and are a rich
source of local information. They list the baptisms, marriages and
burials which took place from then to the present time.

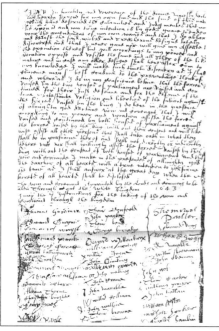

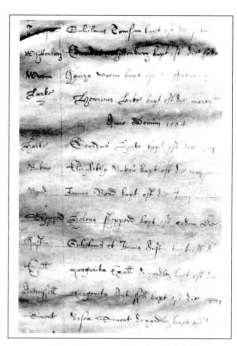

The Vow and Covenant entry of 1643   *Baptism entries for 1564*

Photos: by permission of the Churchwardens of Cottered

Disease

Although somewhat remote, Cottered suffered from time to time with infectious diseases. In 1614, the Rector, the Rev Thomas Bush, explains his absence from some official function by writing the following note.

"Good sir, howbeit I would willingly meet your worship at the place appointed, yet I do think it mete in discretion to forbear, because there having died of late some seventeen persons, the towns abouts do stand in fear of us that we have the infection amongst us, but we hope not. Howbeit we ourselves begin to suspect the disease to be some sort infections."

In the spring of 1782, smallpox raged through the village. At a Vestry Meeting held in March the infection was described as "spreading among the poor inhabitants, which were very numerous." A note was made in the Town Land Account for Cottered, signed by the Rector the Rev Anthony Trollope, grandfather of the famous novelist, and Churchwarden Jeremiah Gutteridge, showing that it had been decided to have all the poor inhabitants inoculated.

The unanimous consent of the Vestry was given in support of this suggestion and to the proposal that "a surgeon should be provided and the expenses paid out of the Town Stock". The surgeon's bill for carrying out the inoculation of the poor amounted to £19s 15s (£19.75), quite a considerable amount at a time when beer was only 2d (1p) a pint and rent of an acre of land was 8s 6d (42p) per annum. The bill put the accounts in 'the red' to the tune of 6s 9d (34p).

Cottered Church

Cottered Parish Church is now dedicated to St John the Baptist, but was once known as St Mary's, according to an early 15th century reference. The church tower, with its impressive tall spire, is the oldest part of the church and dates from the mid 14th century.

The circular shape of the churchyard indicates a pre-Christian site. Lord of the Manor, Richard de Lucie, Justicary of England, who founded Lesnes Abbey, Kent, in 1178, may have built a church here. Richard de Lucie acted as regent when the king was absent from the country. Up until the 15th century, Lesnes Abbey appointed Rectors to the living. The earliest known priest was the Rev William of Canterbury, sub deacon in 1238.

A later Rector was the Rev Angel Chauncy who was responsible for the rebuilding of the spire in 1757 at a cost of £185. He paid £105 towards the bill out of his own pocket. The spire was repaired in the mid 1930's and again in 1962 at a cost of £1,000. Due to beetle infestation and water rot, a £30,000 scheme was begun in 1983 to prevent the spire from collapsing, half the cost being met by the newly formed Friends of Cottered Church.

It has been suggested that Cottered was on a pilgrimage route to Walsingham in Norfolk, which may explain the old 15th century wall painting of St Christopher, the patron saint of travellers, on the wall of the nave opposite the main door of the church. Since the time of the Reformation, the mural was hidden under lime wash. It was discovered during the major repairs of 1886 and restored to its present condition by the Rev Dr. Arthur Granger, Rector from 1915 to 1925.

What remains of the painting is rather difficult to see. St Christopher is depicted carrying the Christ Child, guided by a hermit with a lantern. The background appears to be the local landscape of the period. A few other traces of mediæval paint can be seen, thus suggesting that like most churches of this period Cottered Church was once filled with a blaze of bright colours.

St John the Baptist Church,
Cottered 1983

Andrew Thrussell with the Church
weather vane 1982

Church interior 1975

St Christopher 15th century wall painting 1960's

*Marble font
dated 1739*

There are five bells; the two oldest bells, the Tenor and the Fourth, date from 1650 and 1651 respectively. The newest, the Treble, was cast in 1841. The bells ceased to be rung in 1944 because they had become unsafe, but they were all re-hung in 1962 and ringing was re-established. Eleven years later they were seen and heard on television when the Cottered ringers gave the presenters of 'Magpie', the children's TV programme, a crash course in bell ringing.

The church organ, built by Benjamin Flight and Son in the 1830s, was rebuilt in 1973 at the organ works of Mander's in London.

Fossils from millions of years ago can be seen in the Derbyshire marble font. What happened to the older font, no one knows.

Antony and Jill Edwards with the re-tuned church bells 1962

Stephen Westover who re-guilded
the clock face 1963

The last Church sexton, Fred Darton winds the
church clock 1955

Magpie presenter, Susan Stranks, receives instructions from
Tower Captain, Andrew Thrussell 1973

During the 1950's and 60's, an annual church fete was held at the
Rectory and, in the autumn, a pre-Christmas bazaar in the village
hall to raise funds for the church. For many years there was a
weekly Sunday School with an annual Christmas party and
summer outing, often to Walton-on-the-Naze. The church
therefore provided a network of social occasions. Free beer was
provided for those who, with their scythes and sickles, came
together for the annual mowing of the churchyard.

The church choir, begun in late Victorian times and strong during
the 1950's and 60's, led the singing at services twice on Sundays.
However, the numbers gradually dwindled until the choir ceased
to exist. A re-union of choir members was held in 2003 when
Neville Chuck celebrated fifty years as organist at Cottered.

To mark the Millennium, a new stained glass window was
installed. The congregation chose the scenes used to illustrate the
spreading of the Gospel.

The Millennium window 2001

*The Bishop of St Albans,
the Rt Rev Christopher Herbert
dedicates the window 2001*

Re-union of choir members with Neville Chuck 2003

Throcking Church

Holy Trinity Church, Throcking, dates from the early 13th century and contains memorials by two eminent sculptors of their day, an unusual choir stall carving and consecration crosses. The church is somewhat unusual in that there is no chancel arch. Only a step divides the nave and chancel that are of equal width and height.

The upper portion of the tower was re-built in 1660 by Sir Thomas Soame, whose father Stephen was Lord Mayor of London in 1598-99. Patron and Lord of the Manor, Sir Thomas was Sheriff of London in 1635 and he became an Alderman of the City. He married Joan, a daughter of William Freman of Aspenden. Both are buried in a vault beneath the nave floor.

Made of clunch, a local stone, the 15th century font stands inside the main door. When the Rev William Adams became rector in 1841 he found the Church in a deplorable condition with the font lying broken in the tower.

Rev William Adams

Rector Adams was a great benefactor. At his own expense he re-roofed the Church, repaired the pews and built others to match the 17th century design. When the Rev Adams died in 1878 leaving £500 for "beatifying and repairing" the Church, an organ chamber and vestry were added, the nave windows filled with tinted glass, a pulpit and lectern of wainscot oak erected and deal pews replaced by oak.

The stained glass east window depicts scenes of the 'Good Shepherd'. There is also a notable reredos of Caen stone and an Ippolyt marble super altar. Twelve carved angels once helped support the roof, but they were removed in 1967 because of woodworm.

Gone, too, is the 'plush pulpit cushion and the fringed carpet' the drape for the Communion Table, given by Lord of the Manor Robert Elwes in April 1686. These were both stolen during the County Election Night of 29 April 1736 when intruders broke the window bars, wrenched a chest open and also took 'ye surplice and hood and ye Common Prayer Book' according to an entry in the Church Register.

*15th century font in Throcking Church
1977*

*Acrobats on the choir stall poppyhead
1977*

Holy Trinity Church, Throcking 2005

The large monument to Hester Elwes is by English sculptor Joseph Nollekens (1737 - 1823), whose best-known works are in Westminster Abbey. Sculptor Michael Rysbrack (1693- 1770), carved the monument to Hester's father--in-law, Robert Elwes, and his wife Martha on the south wall of Throcking Church.

The consecration crosses on the wall are said to mark the sites where the Bishop placed Holy Oil when the building was originally dedicated. A 'Poppy Head' at the east end of the north choir stall depicts a group of acrobats and a bird. One man is holding another by his leg, while a man balances upside down on his head.

The first known Rector is Richard de Cruce Roheis (i.e. Royston Cross), in 1216. From then, the patronage descended with the Manor and then to the Rev William Adams, eventually passing to the Bishop of St Albans in 1965.

The parish registers, although poorly kept, contain a list of Briefs. These were Royal Letters sent to the Bishops who in turn sent them to their clergy authorising the collection of alms during Divine Service for specified purposes. Frequently "nothing collected" is recorded. But in 1685, £1 9s (£1.45) was given for a fire in Baldock and the following year £2 12s 6d (£2.62) for French Protestants. In 1716, £2 2s 6d (£2.12) was collected for the Protestant Church in Poland.

The Church once had three bells in the tower, but by 1700 only one remained. This was recast in 1855 and is still in use.

*Robert and Martha Elwes' monument
by Michael Rysbrack 2006*

*Hester Elwes' monument by Joseph
Nollekens 2006*

Harvest Festival at Throcking Church 1967

Robert Elwes Senior gave a "fair house" situated near the Church for the Rectors of Throcking. However, this had completely disappeared by 1808 when it was stated, "no house nor land belonged to the living except the churchyard".

However, in July 1837 work began on a Rectory, built on land given by the Patron, John Ray JP of Finchley. The Rev Adams applied for a £511 grant towards building the Parsonage from the Commissioners of Queen Anne's Bounty, now known as The Church Commissioners.

The building was completed in April the following year and served as The Rectory until it was sold for £1,214 in 1934. The proceeds were used to demolish a wing of the vacant Cottered Rectory and modernise the property. The two Benefices were united in 1932, so only one Rectory was required. Since this period the old Throcking Rectory has been a private house.

The former Rectory at Throcking 2005

Nonconformists

When the new Prayer book first came into force in 1662, all Church of England clergy had to consent to its contents. If they refused they were ejected from their livings. The Rector of Cottered at the time, the Rev Thomas Gardiner was among those who refused and he appeared before the Court, with twenty of his parishioners, for not receiving Communion at the Parish Church.

Under the Toleration Act of 1689, Protestant Nonconformists were allowed to worship openly if their Meeting Houses were licensed. The first licensed Meeting House at Cottered was in 1691. Eight years later, the homes of Edward Browne and of Robert Bennett were both licensed for worship.

A small plot of land to the rear of the cottages opposite The Bull was once the burial ground for the local Quakers, or Society of Friends, as they became known. John Exton, formerly of Ardeley, gave this piece of land at Cottered and he himself was buried there on 23 July 1712. Over the years several burials have taken place there and the Rector of Cottered, the Rev Angel Chauncy, officiated at a number of them. Some of their names are recorded in the Church Burial Registers. It is thought the last burial was in 1826.

Wayside Cottage also seems to have been be used as a Quaker Meeting House. The Manorial Court Roll for 1742 refers to Wayside Cottage as having belonged to the Whittenbury family and in use as a Quakers' Meeting House.

Later, a property in Warren Lane became the Meeting House. In 1808 it was described as "formerly a cottage now used as a Quakers Meeting House." It is currently a boarding kennels.

Quaker burial ground
Commemorative stone
2006

Wayside Cottage, once a Quaker Meeting House, 1900's
Photo loaned by Sally Kingsley

The Meeting House, Warren Lane 1920's
Photo loaned by Jessie Vine

Chapel

A group of Independents, or Congregationalists as they were known, was meeting in Joseph Cooper's barn by 1810. Later a Congregational Chapel was built and served from Buntingford. It was described as a "neat little chapel" in 1856, although it had been unoccupied for four years.

Two years later, Benjamin Culpin was preaching at Cottered every Sunday. He held open-air meetings at first, because the place was dirty and windows were broken. On 11 July that year he held his first service in the chapel and sixty people were present.

The chapel appears to have closed in 1913 but was open again by 1924. A couple of years later, a restoration fund was begun and extensive repairs carried out. In 1934 it closed yet again and became almost derelict. During the Second World War, however, the building was used as the base for the Cottered Home Guard. It was also the Air Raid Precaution post.

In August 1948, the Rev Henry Walker commenced his ministry at the Buntingford Congregational Church and under the new grouping scheme he had charge of several chapels, including Cottered. Mr Walker was very popular and many of his meetings included movie film shows that drew people in.

I was among the teenagers who attended Sunday school at the Parish Church who also went to the chapel services. The Church of England Rector, Rev Joseph Charlton, did not approve, and told us so in no uncertain terms, but we continued going to both. The chapel closed for services for the very last time when Mr Walker moved away in 1951. After this it was used for a variety of purposes, including a library, the Women's Institute and occasionally for Parish Council meetings. The 1st Cottered Guides also met here, and during 1953, Coronation year, a group of youngsters, calling themselves the YIPS (Young Important People's Society), put on a Concert to raise funds.

On Coronation Day itself a television with a large screen was installed to enable local people to watch the ceremony live in black and white.

Eventually the dilapidated Chapel, after being used for storage for some years, was sold. During 1979 it was converted into residential use.

The former Congregational Chapel 1976

YIPS concert in the chapel May 1953

Agriculture

The fertile land in this area, with its springs and small rivers close at hand, no doubt attracted the first settlers to the three parishes.

For many centuries farming was the mainstay of the community and most of the inhabitants worked on or were allied to the land.

The Saxons introduced the Open Field System, under which the largest fields in a village were divided into small strips of land so the good and poor land was shared between all the farmers. Only two out of three fields were cultivated in any one year, the other remained fallow, crops being grown in rotation. The open fields in Cottered consisted of North Field, Church Field, East Field, Hare Field and Peasecroft. Other known fields were Trigwells, Claypit Field and Holbrook.

In the late middle Ages narrow strips of land were allowed to grass over and become common permanent rights of way, called baulks. Farmers were also allowed to graze their cattle on the Lord of the Manor's land. This land consisted of meadows, wasteland and roadside strips. However, cattle were banned from grazing from Candlemas Day, i.e. February 2, until Lamas Day i.e. August 1, when the meadows were cropped. Even from early times, it was an offence to interfere with or cause an obstruction to this common land.

As a result of the various Enclosure Acts at the end of the 18th century and the early 19th century, land was enclosed into fields rather than scattered strips and reallocated to the landowners. In Cottered, this happened around 1810. In 1881 Albert Quilter at The Warren had the largest farm with 392 acres. He employed nine men and three boys to run it. At The Lordship James Maynard farmed 357 acres, employing nine men and four boys. Levi Grant at Childs Farm cultivated 190 acres. He employed six men and three boys. James Bonfield needed four lads and a boy for the 134 acres at Nottingham's.

A pair of traction engines working near Cottered Warren 1959

Threshing at Lodge Hill 1966

At Osbournes Farm (now Cheynes) John Munt employed two men and two boys on his 88 acres. Farming at Flanders Green, Joseph Pearman with 73 acres needed a man and a boy. Smallholder James Cooper at Coles Green Farm had 47 acres and employed a man and a boy.

During this period, then, some 71 Cottered residents were directly engaged in work on the land, representing around 50% of the working population. Another 15% were engaged in the building trade, 15% did domestic work and 8% were living by their own means.

At this time the weekly wage for an agricultural worker was in the region of 17s. (85p). Rent might have accounted for 1s 6d, (7p) butter was 6d a pound, (2p) a loaf of bread two pence and a farthing, (1p) while a pint of beer was 2d. (1p).

Henry Dowton with Kingsley's horses Prince and Punch 1958

Before the arrival of the combine harvester in the mid 20th century, wheat was usually harvested by a group of five. Four reapers with sickles cut the corn and the long stubble left by them was cut with long handled scythes. After the corn was bound, it was left to dry in the fields before being stored and eventually threshed and winnowed. In the 18th century each team member would have harvested one or two acres a day.

Tractor driven binders gave way to combines drawn by tractors. It was not until the 1950's that self-propelled combines were produced. Modern models can cut a swath 30ft wide, harvesting 40 tons an hour.

By the time of the outbreak of the Second World War, weekly agricultural wages for horsemen, cowmen and shepherds were £2 16s 5d (£2.82) while labourers earned £2 8s (£2.40).

Nowadays Cottered no longer has small mixed farms of arable and meadow land with dairy cattle, pigs and poultry. Farms today need fewer people to run them except in the busy times of harvest, when labour is drafted in to cope with the extra demand. Small family farms are disappearing, to be replaced by conglomerates and contract farmers.

Cliff Silver on Smyth's Combine Harvester cutting oats at Throcking
with Wendy Smyth 1959

The present Middle Farm, previously called The Bury, was a mixed arable farm in Throcking from at least the early 19th century. By the middle of the century, it consisted of 176 acres and was farmed by Thomas Cornwell, who had previously farmed and lived at Foxholes. The farm was then bought by the Coleman family of Throcking Hall. It was subsequently farmed by Throcking Churchwarden William Page and then by his nephew Gordon Smyth. Most of the farmland was eventually sold off and the outbuildings, including the early 18th century barn, were converted into a banqueting centre, Bluntswood Hall.

Middle Farm, Throcking 1982

Lower Farm dates from the early 17th century. The first known owner was Nicholas Godfrey, Churchwarden at Throcking. It remained with this family for over a century. Bill and Barbara Murchie, who have farmed here since the time of the Second World War, had great success over a long period showing cattle at major agricultural shows.

Lower Farm, Throcking 1982

Bill Murchie with a Champion's Cup and his prize winning herd 1983
Photo Royston Crow

Local Enterprises

Over the years, with the diversification of agricultural holdings, a number of enterprises have been established. A kennels and cattery has been run at The Meeting House in Warren Lane for nearly fifty years.

Warren Nurseries and The Meeting House Kennels 1994

Warren Lane nursery began by producing chrysanthemums for Covent Garden and later changed to growing bedding plants.

Other enterprises have come and gone. During the 19th century, straw plaiting, a cottage industry, provided extra income for villagers. The plaits were used for making straw hats, with Luton being the main seat of the hat industry. This industry was almost confined to Hertfordshire and the neighbouring counties.

A child could earn 6d (2p) a day plaiting when trade was good, and adults could make between 8s (40p) and 12s (60p) a week. At this period farm labourers earned between 9s and 10s (45p - 50p) a week so a family income could be doubled if the women and children made straw plaits.

According to the Census of 1861 there were more than a dozen straw-plaiters in Cottered. Several plaiters were elderly widows but there were also a few teenagers, including 15-year-old Hephzibar Pickett, the schoolmaster's daughter. Hannah Dilley and Anne Skipp were among the fifteen years olds also engaged in this trade.

However, imports from China at the beginning of 1870s had their effect and the value of the English plait soon fell. Nobody in Cottered was plaiting by the time of the 1871 Census.

Much more recent enterprises include mushrooms and bonsai trees grown at the Old Rectory, Throcking, in the 1950's by the Goldsmiths. Lawntex and flower mats were also produced and some years later, strawberries were grown for Covent Garden. At one period the outbuildings were let for industrial use, as were those at Whytegates Farm, still in existence as Honeywood Industrial Centre.

Other ventures have included Thrussell's Nursery in Potato Field Lane, which produced chrysanthemums, and Stocking Hill Chicken Farm, which has now made way for housing, while Magpie Farm shop, with its free-range chickens and other livestock, has also ceased trading.

Brian Planner with his ostriches 1996
Photo Royston Crow

At one period there was an ostrich farm at Cottered. Brian Planner acquired 40 acres of land at the former Lordship Farm in 1994. Eighteen months later he had more than 70 birds. In the first year there were 50 eggs from each bird, but Brian lost the majority by sending them away to be incubated. So he tried incubating them by putting the eggs in a greenhouse, which was more successful. However, the ostrich farm only lasted a few years and the land is now grazed by cattle.

Tradesmen

In the middle of the nineteenth century, Cottered had a wide variety of trades people. Among those listed in a directory of 1855 are George Beadle carpenter, Joseph Camp wheelwright and blacksmith, Thomas Cox and Thomas Grant shoemakers, George Mole and Fanny Smith shopkeepers. About ten years later the names also included John Hurry, shopkeeper, Walter Beamiss, plasterer and John King, dairyman.

Ted Newman
the last village
blacksmith

Thatcher Jonah Brown appeared before the Buntingford Magistrates in 1898 for being asleep and without a light whilst in charge of a horse and cart in the High Street, Buntingford. He was ordered to pay a 2s 6d (12p) fine with 4s (20p) costs.

There were two village cobblers in the early twentieth century. One was Joe Woods of Wayside Cottage, whose wife was deaf and dumb. The other cobbler was "Snob" Walter Hummerston who was deaf and resided at what is now 2 Lilac Cottages.

There was a blacksmiths at The Old Forge between Lower Farm and the school, with Joe Warner as the blacksmith, employed by wheelwright William Reed.

The Forge and Wheelwright's in the centre of Cottered 1900's
Photo loaned by Sally Kingsley

William Reed

Joe Warner later had his own blacksmith's shop near the rear of the chapel. Ted Newman took over from him and was the last of our village blacksmiths.

The Reed family came to Cottered in 1892. William had several sons who took it in turns to help the blacksmith, moving on to become an apprentice wheelwright with their father. After serving in the First World War, two of the sons started the builder's business and expanded with new premises at the eastern end of the village in 1932. They ceased trading in 1989.

One of William's daughters, Dorothy, recalled:

Reeds' invoice 1936

"Father used to put new tyres on the farm carts. He used to light a big fire near the Blacksmith's shop. When the iron tyres were red hot, long pincers were used to carry them and put them over the wooden wheel. Then he used to bang it on with long handled hammers. Then cans of water were poured round to cool the rim. When the fire has burnt to ashes, the children used to put potatoes in their skins to cook and afterwards rake them out. They tasted so good!"

Reeds' workshop 1982

The village once had its own builders and undertakers. The Beadle family served the village in these capacities until the end of the Second World War.

Charles Beadle and Emily Pearman on their wedding day 1894
Photo loaned by Vera Slazak

The Cole and Bygrave premises, previously Beadles' Workshop, 1950's
Photo loaned by Den Thorp

The latest use of the same premises, Cottered Service Station 1991

Left to right: Ted Newman, Joe Warner, Frances Warner, Joan Gray
and Glad Gray at the petrol pumps 1927
Photo loaned by Shirley Fowler

The Beadles' old workshop was purchased in 1952 by Cole & Bygrave and transformed into a car and bodywork repairs business. Den Thorp's garage in turn replaced them ten years later. Petrol could be obtained from pumps outside what is now Cheyenne, then from Arthur Burr at the same place, before they were moved to their present site at Cottered Service Station in 1967.

Arthur Burr

Taxi services were provided by farmer Frank Charles, publican Frank Lawman and shopkeeper Alan Edwards at various periods. The haulage firm C Charles & Sons, based at Osbournes Farm, continues to serve a wide area.

The Skipp family was well known in the area and far beyond the village for their rag trade business. The first mention of the Skipp family at Cottered appears to be in the late 18th century when a William Skipp was baptised. Fanny Skipp was among the first intake of pupils at Cottered School when it opened in 1829. Thomas Skipp, a butcher, lived at Green Gates, Brook End in 1901. His son Ernest began the rag and bone business and he travelled the district with his pony and cart, exchanging oranges

Ernest, Florence and Emily Skipp outside Strawberry Cottage 1900's
Photo loaned by Lou Skipp

for rabbit skins. With the help of his sons the business grew into scrap metal dealing. Now the business is that of scrap metal and the supply of logs.

Fred Pepper delivered greengrocery around the village and there were other tradesmen from outside the village delivering fresh fish, bread, meat, vegetables and, on Saturday evenings, fish and chips.

Milk once came from dairy herds in the village. With the aid of a horse, Blossom, and cart, Walter Ross and Land girl Ethel Gaunt delivered milk to parts of the village, while Frank Charles of Little Osbournes used his car to deliver to the rest.

Dick Knight took over both milk rounds and, with the help of his sister, Mary, and his wife, Eileen, continued to deliver milk until they retired in 1978. In more than 30 years they reckoned they only let their customers down once when their supply failed to reach them because of snow. On another occasion, when Cottered was cut off by snow drifts in 1958, the couple bought milk from local farmers and delivered it direct from the milk churns into whatever receptacle their customers could find.

Dick and Eileen also had a newspaper round, while the resourceful

Peter and Hilda Knight, Robin Meekins and
Mary Knight with 'Tommy' 1950's
Photo loaned by Peter Knight

Eileen ran errands for customers and even washed their hair and cut their toenails! Dave and Ros Charles took on the milk and paper round in 1978 and continued until the end of 2001.

Frank Charles with his horse 1920's
Photo loaned by Derek Charles

Eileen and Dick Knight 1978

Ros Charles delivers the milk during the snow 1979

Key:

1. Nottingham Farm	8. Ivy Cottage	15. Lower Farm
2. Lilac Cottages	9. The Bell	16. Telephone Exchange
3. The Kennels	10. Chapel	17. Blacksmiths &
4. Paddocks Wells	11. Bowling Green Farm	wheelwrights
5. Childs Farm	12. The White House	18. School old
6. Off Licence	13. The Nook	19. School new & Guide HQ
7. Town House	14. Green View Cottage	20. The Bull

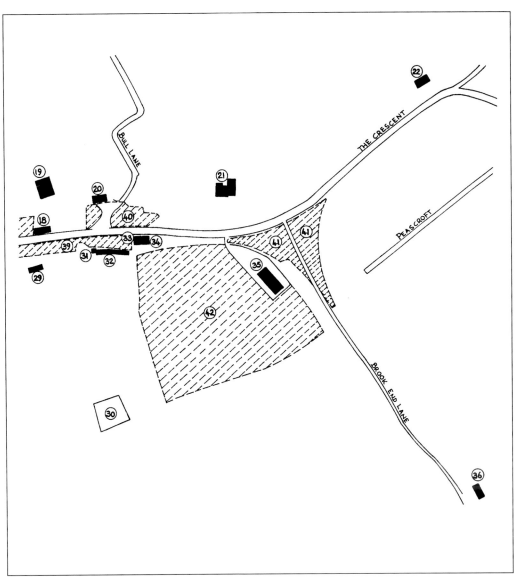

21. The Old Rectory
22. Magpie Farm
23. Cheynes Barn
24. Cheynes Farm
25. The Rectory
26. Cottered Church
27. The Lordship
28. Village shop & PO

29. Shipwrights
30. Quaker Burial Ground
31. Cartwright's shop
32. Home Close
33. Flint Cottage
34. Wayside Cottage
35. Village Hall
36. Greengates

37. Japanese Gardens
38. Bowling Green
39. The Green
40. Bull Green
41. Cross Green
42. Playing Field

Map drawn by Jo Hayden

Public Houses

For many years Cottered had two pubs and an off licence and technically speaking Throcking also had a pub, although it was situated in Buntingford, part of which was then Throcking parish.

Bull Green and The Bull (right) 1900's
Photo loaned by Carol Clark

The Bull at Cottered may have had Edward Bull as its first landlord. His name is mentioned in 1599 when his son Richard was baptised at Cottered Church. Another Edward Bull, a butcher, appeared before the Quarter Sessions in 1634, for throwing up 'heaps of dirte or soyle' on the highway. In 1644 Mary Bull, a widow, also appeared before the Quarter Session for giving short measure of ale.

By the beginning of the 18th Century, The Bull had evidently become the regular meeting place for the Town Meetings where the general business of the parish was carried out. These were apparently far from dull affairs as the accounts show that Mary Hine received a guinea (£1.05) and Widow Herbert 1s (5p) for drink.

Frank Lawman Jr

William Baker, who was landlord in 1880, was also a butcher. He appeared before the magistrates for 'corroded scales' used to weigh out pork and flour.

In the early 1930's Frank Lawman senior took over the pub, helped by his wife Rose. After his death, Rose took on the license and eventually Frank junior their son, who was there until he retired in 1976.

He was followed by Michael & Rita Ward and then Gerry and Elaine Wilson in 1993. After they left, Tom Burley took over in 1995 and carried out major renovations with an emphasis on restaurant meals.

The Bull 1930's
Photo loaned by Joyce Cartwright

The other Cottered pub, The Bell, was once called 'The Chequers'. It was known by this name in 1724 when Thomas Dearmer of Ickleford and Elizabeth Draper of The Chequers were married at Cottered Church.

Members of the Beadle family kept the pub from the early eighteenth century for nearly a hundred years. Some of them held other jobs; for example, William Beadle was also a wheelwright. By the 1860's Sarah Cooper was the tenant.

The occupiers in the 1930's were the Phillips family, whose daughter Doreal married Barry Lupino, one of England's best known theatrical performers.

The Bell 1950's

*Reg and Eve
Handisyde*

Among the more recent landlords were Bob and Vera Neilson, who took over the pub in 1952 and Reg and Eve Handisyde in the 1960's.

Greene King, who already owned The Bull, then acquired The Bell and put in managers John and Carol Clarke. The Clarkes left in July 1990 after which the property was de-licensed and sold as a private dwelling.

The Adam and Eve pub, near Buntingford Roman Catholic Church, stood for centuries on land that was once part of Throcking parish. After the pub closed, the property was demolished in 1969 and replaced by the Adam & Eve Filling Station. This has since been knocked down to make way for residential development

Almost opposite The Bell in Cottered is the Old Off Licence, where beer was served for over a century. By 1835 the property was described as a 'beer house' and owned by Phillips, the Royston brewery family. David Field, a shoemaker, and his wife Rachel lived here. Thomas Grant, another shoemaker, lived here in the mid nineteenth century with his son Levi and his daughter Lucy, who married William Kingsley. In 1904 William was fined for having 'unjust measures, one pint and one half pint'.

Eventually sisters Mary "Polly" Kingsley and Alice Emerton had the Off Licence. After Mary died in 1937, Ted and Ivy Newman, who had recently married, moved in and took over the business. Then in the early 1950s, Ted purchased the property from the brewery and since then it has been a private house.

The Old Off Licence 1950's

Ted Newman and Ivy Cartwright on their wedding day 1936
Photo loaned by Joyce Cartwright

Shops

The village once had several shops. George Mole and his wife Anna had a general stores at The White House around 1890 and at the rear of the premises was a bakery where Harold and Wat Beamiss baked "good bread" before the outbreak of the First World War. The shop was licensed to sell tobacco and snuff.

On his way to school between 1913 and 1921, farmer's son Percy Kingsley used to buy 'one penny worth of sweets' from Hannah Smith's shop at 2 Home Close. At one time there was also a shop at Flint Cottage, run by 'Tot' Mean and another at The Old Forge where Monte and Glad Gray sold fruit and vegetables.

The main shop in the village was opened during the First World War by Joe Warner, the village blacksmith. Alan Edwards acquired the shop in 1923. A butcher by trade, he had been advised to leave Walthamstow in East London and move to the country for 'health reasons'.

Alan Edwards outside his shop late 1920's.
Photo loaned by Den Thorp

The shop at this time occupied what is now the living room of Green View Cottage, and much of the stock was kept on the stairs. A wooden extension was later added to the front of the cottage to accommodate the shop.

In the 1930's, Alan Edwards bought part of the Lordship orchard from William Sanders for £100, on which he built a new shop and Post Office with living accommodation.

Much of the produce sold was local, with fresh butter from Bowling Green Farm and salt butter from Childs Farm. Honey was produced from Mr Edwards' own bees and pickled pork came from his own pigs.

The Edwards used to have a black Labrador dog called Simon. On the days that the Wall's van was due to deliver, and only on those days, the dog sat outside waiting for it to come, as the driver would give him any broken pieces of pastry.

Jim Edwards and with his younger brother Dick ran the shop jointly until 1977 when Dick left. Jim remained until 1982, when he retired and the business was sold.

The Shop and Post Office 1958

Christmas time at Edwards' shop 1960's
L to r. Mary Knight, Florrie Dunn, Valerie Gray, Jim and Dick Edwards

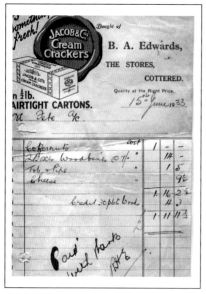

Bill for Edwards' shop 1933

The new owners, Alan Monk and his wife Linda, had previously owned a fish and chip shop in Baldock. The business then changed hands several times and, like most village shops, found it difficult to make a profit. It closed on Village Day 1987, while in the ownership of Peter and Rose Shepherd.

New owners, Jeremy and Janet Stephens, reopened the shop on Village Day 1989. However, in spite of their efforts, the shop finally closed in August 1991.

A delivery van calls at Cartwright's shop (far right) 1950's

As well as B. A. Edwards & Sons, a smaller shop, Cartwright's, was run by Percy and Elizabeth Cartwright at 4 Home Close, where children could once buy "loose sherbet for a penny."

When Percy was in his garden, customers had to wait for him to come in to serve. There was always a quaint smell of paraffin, tobacco and sweets. Cartwright's opened on Sunday mornings, but Edwards' didn't.

"Mrs Cartwright used to sell loose tobacco in a jar. The old men would come down for their half ounce of shag regularly every week," recalls her daughter-in-law, Joyce Cartwright. "She would then weigh it out and wrap it up in newspaper for them."

After Percy's death, Elizabeth continued with the business until it closed around 1968.

Elizabeth Cartwright

The Post Office

Cottered's postal history appears to date from 1855 when a hand stamp for the village was issued. Towards the end of the 19th century the Post Office was at Flint Cottage. William Pickett was sub-master by 1863 and he was also Head of Cottered School from 1829 until his death in 1874. His daughter Hephzibar was in charge of the Post Office in 1878.

Post Office at Flint Cottage 1959

Post Office at Ivy Cottage
next to The Bell 1907
Photo loaned by Joyce Cartwright

In 1879 the Post Office moved to Ivy Cottage, where Park House now stands. Walter Beamiss was in charge in 1882 and he was succeeded by his daughter, Annie Beamiss, who for sixty years was also organist at Cottered Church.

The White House, once a Post Office, shop and bakery 1900's
Photo loaned by Jessie Vine

It was about this period that the Post Office was transferred to
The White House where it remained until it moved to The Nook.
By 1922 Frances Beadle was the sub postmistress. She was also
an organist, this time of Throcking Church.

Cottered Post Office when it was located at The Nook 1920's
Photo loaned by Joyce Cartwright

The Post Office was at the Village Stores until the shop closed in 1987 after which it moved to the Village Hall where it operated on two mornings each week under the charge of Jo Baird until 2003. Had it not been for her involvement, it is likely that Cottered, like so many other villages, would have lost its Post Office.

Postmistress Jo Baird 1987

Elsie Dowton

Among the villagers who delivered the mail in Cottered were Percy Cartwright and Kenneth Pugh. Kenneth had a family of sixteen children and lived in a three-bedroom council house. Elsie Dowton, another post lady, known affectionately as 'Elsie the Post', kept biscuits in the pocket of her uniform to pacify any dogs on her route. The last village postwoman was Betty Chapman. Mail is now delivered by van from outside the parish.

Betty Chapman makes her last mail delivery 1983
Photo Royston Crow

The School

Cottered School early 1900's
Photo loaned by Sally Kingsley

Founded some 40 years before State Education was introduced, the village school was established in 1825 by Henry Soames, a London tallow chandler who resided at Broadfield Hall. The Lord of the Manor, Dr Richard Forrester, allowed a two-roomed school building to be erected on part of the village green in 1829.

Two teachers were appointed, William Pickett and Ann Gutteridge, each receiving a salary of £20 a year from rents on buildings in Cheapside and Bow Lane, London. The next Lord of the Manor, local timber merchant Robert Wilkins, sold some land to provide a playground at the rear of the school. Later, he also granted a strip of land so that a third classroom could be built at the western end of the building.

Jessie Anable

By the time I went to Cottered School, the staff had been reduced to two, Florence Ross and Jessie Anable. They taught the entire curriculum between them. Mrs Ross, who lived at The Place, was Headmistress from 1931 to 1951. She taught Years 4 to 7 in one classroom, while Miss Anable taught what is now Years 1 to 3 in the other. Miss Anable was a teacher at the school from 1911 until 1950. They had no help, except for textbooks and, from 1948 onwards, schools broadcasts on the newly acquired radio. There was no staff room or head's office. During play and lunch times one of the teachers had to remain on duty.

Pupils at Cottered School with Headmistress Florence Ross 1946
Photo loaned by Margaret Ward

Pupils took the 11 plus exam for Grammar School. I passed, but decided to go to a secondary modern school instead. Some children eventually went into teaching and other professions. Others emigrated to New Zealand and Australia, South America and the USA, but most, like me, remained in the village all their working lives.

The premises became unsuitable for the needs of the school and eventually, with the backing of the Cottered School Association in 1970, a letter was sent to Margaret Thatcher, then Minister of Education. These efforts were finally rewarded and a new school was promised.

After a number of setbacks, building work began. One of the main features of the £70,000 project was the unusual pyramid style roof.

Teacher Sarah Leaver and pupils at the new school building 1975

The new school building could accommodate up to 75 pupils. It had a well-equipped kitchen, with dual-purpose hall/gymnasium. Pupils moved in during November 1974, although workmen were still on the site. The building was officially opened on 25 March 1975 by the Rt. Rev Robert Runcie, Bishop of St Albans who was enthroned as Archbishop of Canterbury exactly five years later. Former pupils were sad to see the old School demolished to make way for a car park.

The School marked its 150th anniversary in 1979 with a two-day celebration. Almost everyone dressed up in Victorian costume, including Lt Col Robin Soames, the great-great grandson of the founder, who attended.

Eventually the School ceased to be viable. Inspite of a gallant fight by parents, including TV coverage, the school, with only four pupils remaining, closed on 16 December 1992. In losing its school, Cottered lost a vital focal point for its community.

The Bishop of St Albans, the Right Rev Robert Runcie, dedicates the new school, watched by pupils and the Rector of Cottered, the Rev Jeff Stratton 1975

The last Head Teacher, Ann Taylor, staff members and final four pupils 1992
Photo Royston Crow

The building remained empty and unsold until 1996. It then became the new County Headquarters of the Hertfordshire Guides. In its new capacity, the premises are once again used by children from all over the County.

Opening of the Guide Headquarters by Chief Guide
Commissioner for Anglia, Vivienne Scouse May 1997
Photo Royston Crow

A pre-school 'Jumping Jacks' was opened in September 1997 at the Guide Centre with six children. Under its leader, Lynne Premadasa, it has grown and can now cater for nearly thirty children aged between two and five years.

Buildings

Most of the old buildings in the parish are timber framed and many are thatched. The Lordship is thought to be the oldest house in Cottered, built about 1428 by Sir John Fray. The house still has its moat on two sides. The internal panelling is Jacobean and there is also a chimneypiece of this period. Part of an old brew house also remains. Major Gwilym Lloyd-George, son of former Prime Minister David Lloyd-George, lived at The Lordship in the 1950's. It was while he was Home Secretary that he made the decision, sitting in his study, that Ruth Ellis should hang. She was the last woman to be hanged in Britain. Gwilym Lloyd-George was created Lord Tenby in 1957.

Shipwrights may have once been the Home Farm of the Lordship Estate, but has been much altered over the years.

"Granny" Jane Smith outside Shipwrights 1920's
Photo loaned by Shirley Wilson

Cheynes Farm was formerly known as Osbournes and known by that name when yeoman Philip Antwissell owned it in the 16th century. In 1896, it was sold to the Rev Henry Izod Rogers for £1,740. At that time it had a dairy and cellar.

Lord Tenby 1961

Lady Tenby 1961

Nottingham Farm 1991

Nottingham Farm is a 17th century house, but no longer a farm. In 1879, thirteen-year-old Jane Barnes of Sandon, a domestic servant at Nottingham Farm, was tried at the Herts Assizes for setting fire to a barn on the property. She was acquitted on the grounds that she had no proper knowledge of right or wrong. The wood and slate wheat barn and also the stables and other buildings, including two cottages, were destroyed by fire.

Tragedy also struck the Parker family who resided here in 1910. Violet, the 14-month-old daughter of the farm bailiff, accidentally hanged herself on the farm gate, when her bonnet caught in the gate hook.

Bowling Green Farm 2005

Bowling Green Farm, formerly known as Hastie's Farm, dates from around 1500. This half-timbered building, with its typical mediæval layout, overlooks the main village green and is now a private house.

Rumbolds 1920's
Photo loaned by Ethel Gaunt

Rumbolds was the home for some years of heart surgeon Donald Ross. It dates from the early 16th century.

Childs Farm is probably even older and is referred to as 'Childs' in records dated 1678. In 1775 the farm was part of the Broadfield Estate. It has been occupied by the Kingsley family since the beginning of the twentieth century.

Childs Farm 1950's

Little Osbournes Farm dates from the mid nineteenth century and is still a working farm and the base for a haulage business. Whytegates Farm, built in 1939 for £472, has now diversified away from agricultural use.

Little Osbournes Farm 1920's
Photo loaned by Jessie Vine

Whytegates Farm 1940's
Photo loaned by Francis Ridley

Broom Manor at Hare Street dates from the 16th century with its brick front being added in 1700. It was once the home of General Sir Frederick Pile, head of the Anti-Aircraft Command during the Battle of Britain.

General Pile

Broom Manor 1988

Paddocks Wells and The Kennels 1920's
Photo loaned by Joyce Cartwright

Former almshouse, Paddocks Wells, was rebuilt in its present position in 1691. Next to it stands The Kennels, once the home of Scottish surgeon Sir James Cantlie, who established a College of Medicine for the Chinese in Hong Kong. One of his students was Dr. Sun Yat Sen, later to become the first President of China in 1912. When Dr. Sun was taken prisoner at the Chinese Legation in London in 1896, it was through James Cantlie's intervention that he was released. A bronze tablet bust of Sir James Cantlie was unveiled by Miss A Sze, daughter of a former Chinese Minister to Great Britain, at Cottered Church.

Lower Farm, Cottered and the Village Well 1961

Lower Farm, Cottered and Coles Green Farm both date from the 16th century. Coles Green Farm was once part of the Broadfield Estate, as was Cottered Warren.

Other notable older buildings include the row of cottages called Home Close, Rosemary and Sherrington cottages. The almshouses, now called Town House, were built in the eighteenth century.

Left. to right: Sam, James, Sarah, Maggie and Annie Cooper
outside Coles Green Farm 1920's
Photo loaned by Joyce Cartwright

Cottered Warren, once part of a larger estate 1976

Home Close in the early 1900's
Photo loaned by Carol Clark

Rosemary Cottages at the bottom of The Alley 1920's
Photo loaned by Sally Kingsley

Sherrington Cottage (right) 1900's
Photo loaned by Sally Kingsley

The Almshouses 1905
Photo loaned by Joyce Cartwright

More recent buildings include the Victorian style rectory opposite the Playing Field which became a private house when a new rectory was built near the church in 1967. The first example of purpose built homes for workers is the row of four terraced brick cottages known as Victoria Cottages, built in 1887.

The Victorian Rectory in the early 1900's before the east wing was demolished.
Photo loaned by Jessie Vine

Victoria Cottages built in 1887
Photo by Steve Auckland 2003

Since the end of the First World War, ninety local authority homes have been built as well as a number of private houses. The early council houses, The Crescent, were built in the 1920's and mid 30's.

The Crescent 1920's
Photo loaned by Carol Clark

The Crescent 'New Road' 1961

Immediately after the Second World War, when materials were scarce, pre-fabricated timber buildings, known as the Swedish Houses, were built in Peasecroft. Other houses, including the flats were added over the years.

The Swedish Houses, Peasecroft 1960's
Photo by Steve Auckland 2003

Peasecroft flats in 1992

As farming changed over the last twenty years, many historical farm barns were no longer needed for their original purpose. Among these barns are sixteenth century buildings at The Lordship and The Warren which have been converted to residential use.

A mid 1930's barn conversion, Lordship Farm (foreground) 1960.

Barn conversions at Cottered Warren 2006

Other recent executive homes have been erected on the site previously used by Reeds the builders.

In 1952, part of the Glebe land belonging to the Church Commissioners was purchased to provide a site for a Village Hall and a playing field. Much of the building of the Village Hall was carried out by local volunteers and the hall was completed and opened in January 1957.

By the 1990's the hall was becoming too expensive to repair and the Management Committee began to plan for a new hall. A substantial Lottery grant, together with other grants and considerable local fundraising, provided the means to build an impressive new hall in 2001.

The old Village Hall 1957

The new Village Hall 2006

Village Greens

T he village greens are an attractive feature of Cottered. The green at the junction to Brook End is known as Cross Green, where there once stood a cross, still shown on a map of 1766. The green in front of The Bull is known as Bull Green. Opposite and further westwards is known simply as The Green.

The main triangular green between the Baldock and Walkern roads is called Bowling Green. It was known by this name as early as 1853, but when, or if, bowls were ever played on it, no one really knows. However, quoits were played here during the early part of the 20th century. At this time, quoits were usually horseshoes thrown at a pin in the ground. This is probably where the whipping posts and stocks stood.

There were several court cases during the mid 19th century involving the felling of trees on the greens. Villagers and the Lords of the Manor were in dispute about the right to fell the trees. In 1861, timber merchant Robert Bird Wilkins, the owner of Cottered Manor, decided to cut down some trees on the village green. Villagers opposed the felling of the trees and the first day's proceedings resulted in a drawn battle. On the following morning all the labourers' wives were persuaded to sit down round the trees, successfully stopping any attempt to cut them down. When the matter was taken to court, the judge decided that the trees did not belong to the Lord of the Manor, as whatever grew on the common belonged to the commoners.

Bowling Green in 1961

It was claimed that there had been hooks in the trees for the women to fix their clotheslines to as long as could be remembered.

For generations an old elm tree with a large burr on its trunk stood on Bowling Green. Known as "Bumpy," it attracted visitors from far and wide until it was felled under cover of darkness during the early hours of 5 November 1929.

The unexpected felling of the tree so upset the villagers that they went straight to the village shop for paraffin with which to burn the fallen tree. The villagers obviously thought that, as they were too late to save the tree, they would make sure no one could benefit from its anticipated sale. The burr would have made the tree valuable for furniture making.

A special meeting of Cottered Parish Council was held and Mr William Sanders, son of the Lord of the Manor Ralph Erskine Sanders, addressed the meeting. He claimed that he and his brothers had tried to prevent the tree from being taken down and thought all was settled. The chairman of the parish council met the Lord of the Manor to see if an amicable settlement could be found.

Bumpy Tree 1920's
Photo loaned by Joyce Cartwright

Lord of the Manor Ralph Sanders
Photo Royston Crow

Some of the villagers with the felled tree 1929
Photo loaned by Dick Edwards

At the next parish council meeting, Ralph Sanders offered the Green to Cottered Parish Council, thus giving up some of his manorial rights. The parish council accepted, and agreed to forego any claim to Bumpy tree. A handing over ceremony took place at The Lordship in April 1931 when the Deeds were given to the parish council.

The greens have been used for village events over the years, such as the travelling fair on St John the Baptist day and Maypole dancing. The fair ceased to be an annual event in 1964.

Maypole dancing on the Village Green 1948
Photo by George Mathers

Gwen Newman, Cottered's May Queen in 1949
Photo loaned by Frankie Richardson

The annual fair 1959

The Puckeridge Hunt meets on Bowling Green 1961

The Millennium Shelter 2001

The village well once stood on Bowling Green but it was filled in during the 1960's. A replica shelter was built to mark the Millennium. It was opened in February 2001 by Sally Kingsley, former chairperson of the Parish Council, and former resident Antony Edwards, in memory of his parents.

Village Day

Cottered's annual Village Festival was first launched in 1986 under the auspices of the Friends of Cottered Church, who raise money for the upkeep of the parish church. Local organisations combine to raise funds for their own activities at what has become the major social event of the year.

Elaine Hornett, Miss Anglia, arrives with Harold Newman
to open the first Village Day 1986
Picture: Royston Crow

Dancers outside The Bull Village Day 2000
Photo Royston Crow

Car boot sale Village Day 2001

Village Day 2004

Best Kept Village

After entering the annual Best Kept Village competition for almost thirty years, Cottered at last won the small village section for the first time in 1989 and then went on to win it for the following three years.

The Lord Lieutenant of Hertfordshire, Simon Bowes Lyon, the Queen's cousin, carried out the unveiling of the sign ceremony on each occasion.

"One of Cottered's great challenges, a main A-road running through the centre of the village, makes the job of keeping the village clean a difficult one," observed Simon Bowes-Lyon. In 1990, in addition to Cottered winning the award, Throcking was placed third in the hamlets section and also received a certificate.

In 1991, for being the village with the highest marks in the area, Cottered also won the 'Hertfordshire Mercury Rose Bowl'.

Lord Lieutenant of Hertfordshire, Simon Bowes-Lyon,
unveils Cottered's Best Kept Village sign 1989

The War Years

Seven Cottered men gave their lives in the service of their country during the First World War. They were Sidney Barker, who was shot during a charge to take Hill 60 in Belgium, when he was just 22 years old. Samuel Castle (33), Patrick Seymour (22), Clement Parker (25), John Pinnock (30), Cecil Smith (18) and Herbert Wilds (19) were all killed in France.

Patrick Seymour

In a letter from the front, Lance Corporal Watt Beamiss who lived at The White House, wrote, "At 5.30 a.m. on 19 December 1915, the enemy attempted a gas attack. The gas makes one feel very sick and if it gets into the eyes they are painful and watery." Watt was taken prisoner in Germany the following April, and wrote to his sister, "You will no doubt be wondering what has become of me. I was taken prisoner on 19 April with a few more. We had a rough time but are lucky to still be living. I have lost everything except my Prayer Book."

During this period, the children from Cottered School sent out socks, mittens and other items for the soldiers.

When the war was over, the returning servicemen, together with the special constables, were provided with a special supper in Cheynes Barn. There was roast beef, with ham and pickles followed by plum pudding and mince pies. Thomas Stick from Cottered Warren provided beer and Herbert and Constance Goode gave bananas, apples, sweets, crackers and cigarettes.

The Second World War had an even greater impact on the village, although only three local men lost their lives in the fighting. These were Frederick Jackson who died on 9 June 1940 aged 33, Percy Hummerston (26) who died on 19 August 1943 and who had worked on the notorious Burma/Siam Railway as a Prisoner of War, and Ernest Hayden who died on 11 June 1945 aged 24.

First World War recruitment poster

More than one and a half million British people, mostly children, were moved out of cities and towns in September 1939 as it was thought they would be safer in the country. Some of them were sent to Cottered.

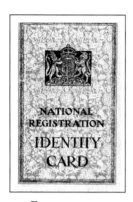

Everyone was issued with an identity card

Florence Ross, then Head Mistress of Cottered School, noted: "Children sent out of London to friends living in the village have been admitted and the empty classroom is being used by girls from North Hackney Central School under their own teachers."

Their Headmistress, Miss G F Hole, writing at the time says, "It was a plunge into the unknown. For the first time in my life, I boarded a train with 231 children, under such sealed orders, that the driver alone knew our destination. Small brothers and sisters presented a very real problem. They were an added responsibility to the staff and too great a burden to the elder girls in whose charge they had been placed by their parents. For preference they had to be separated from their Central School sisters and accommodated in the village schools."

There was little disruption to life in the village until 1940 when air raids began, affecting school lessons and church services. In July 1940, another eighty evacuees came to the village. The school had to share its premises with so many evacuees that local children attended in the mornings and the evacuees in the afternoons.

Numerous villagers were involved in the war effort as ARP Wardens, Special Constables and Firemen. Cottered had its own Fire Service with an appliance known as the 'Cottered Firebug', consisting of a trailer and a pump, kept in the large barn at Lower Farm. When Buntingford Fire Brigade were attending fires in London, Cottered's appliance was on standby. There was also a local Home Guard, or 'Dad's Army', who met in the Congregational chapel.

During 1940, an unexploded parachute mine fell at Cottered, not far from The Meeting House in Warren Lane and villager Frank Hummerston is said to have cut the cord off the parachute.

Six high explosive bombs fell in October that year, killing one of Kingsley's horses as well as a crow and a rabbit near the Searchlight Unit next to the old Chalk Pit at Lodge Hill. Some of the Unit's buildings still remain, including the Officers' Mess, a wooden hut which is now one of the outbuildings at Paddocks Wells. The hut was used to house Cottered's first playgroup in the late 1960's. Another ten high explosive bombs fell at Lower Farm, Throcking in November, but there were no casualties.

Evacuee children from Gipsy Road School, South Norwood arrived in January 1941. They were merged with the Cottered School pupils and some lessons were held in Cheynes Barn. The barn was later used as a workshop making parachutes for the Letchworth firm of Irvin Airchutes. A number of local women were employed here.

In March 1943, the Women's Institute committee started a centre at The Lordship to distribute cod liver oil and fruit juices. The committee also arranged for baths for the soldiers billeted at the Searchlight Unit. Members also knitted garments for children in Europe. Land Girls were posted to farms in the village, some of whom never left.

*Recruitment poster
for the
Land Army*

Bomb damage throughout the war was light, although twenty Council Houses were slightly damaged when a bomb fell in a field about a mile southeast of the village in March 1945.

Thanksgiving services were held at Cottered Church to mark the end of the war and the W.I. organised a Victory Tea for 130 children in May 1945, followed by sports on the green. Other VE celebrations in the village included a campfire at The Lordship and a big bonfire on Cross Green where an effigy of Hitler was burned.

*Brass altar cross commemorating
those killed in the First World War*

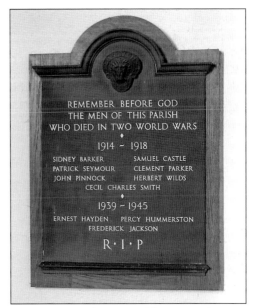

*Remembrance tablet erected
in Cottered Church*

Cottered Organisations

The earliest mention of Cottered Cricket Club is in 1878 when the local lads played against Buntingford. By 1882 Otto Strauss of The Kennels was the team captain and matches were played in a field belonging to James Maynard of The Lordship. In 1894 the Cottered team had no less than three Nottinghamshire players (Richard P Daft, H R Daft and G Stubbs). Their captain at the time was the Rev Henry Izod Rogers.

The club organised a grand Fete to raise club funds in July 1924, but one of the club officials made off with the proceeds! At one period home matches were played in Eight Acres, later to become the site of Magpie Farm. The present playing field has been used by the club since 1927.

Cottered cricket team 1964

*Left to right (back row) Brian Liles, Eric Chamberlain, Ray Charles,
Ken Ward, Fred Pinnock, David Aldridge
(Front row) John Hughes, Arthur Woods, Bert Cartwright (captain.),
Frank Hummerston and Terry McGrath*

The late 1980's and early 1990's were particularly successful for the club. The team picked up the Mill Sports League Title for the fifth time in six seasons, retained the Thundridge Cup for five years and also won the Keatley Cup several times.

In July 1993 a new Pavilion and Clubhouse was opened by club member Nick Whitehead. The Pavilion was later extended to meet the standards imposed by the Farren Herts Cricket League which the club joined, following promotion.

Cottered Football Club's history is somewhat chequered, both in its achievements and records. It is said that Percy Cartwright began the club between the two World Wars.

The successful football team 1931

Back row (left to right) Sid Vine, Will Turner, Fred Woods, Walter Savage, Billy Patmore,
Frank Lawman Sr., Phil Vine, Jack King, Frank Lawman Jr.,
Middle row: Tom Skipp, Les Gilbert, Albert Vine, Stanley Shepherd, Sam Savage, Vic Ginn,
Front row: Jack Vine, Norman Shepherd, Ted Newman, Dan Pinnock and George Miles.
Photo loaned by Ted Newman

Soon after the end of the Second World War the Club was playing in the North Herts League. After a lapse, the club re-started in 1961 and nine years later was fielding a Sunday team in addition to the Saturday teams.

England Captain Emlyn Hughes was the Club's president for some years. Cottered became Champions of the Premier Division of the League in 1982. Three years later, the club built their own Pavilion with changing rooms and a clubroom and volunteers carried out much of the building work. It was opened by their president Gordon Smyth. The pavilion was demolished in 2001 to make way for the new Village Hall which incorporated modern facilities for the club.

Members of the Welcome Club at Toppesfield 1989

Cottered Welcome Club for senior citizens was founded in 1980 and still meets regularly at the village hall for talks and games such as darts and dominoes. Club members chat over a cup of tea and at Christmas they enjoy a meal together at a local pub or restaurant.

A flourishing Petanque Club now has its own piste on the Playing Field at Cottered.

The Horticultural Society was founded in 1942 to encourage the 'Dig for Victory' campaign by growing food. Farmer Tom Kingsley was the first chairman. The Society also held fund-raising events both for the first village hall and for its more recent replacement. Former Society's presidents include Lord Tenby and Prince Georg of Denmark. The Society organizes outings which are very popular with members and friends and holds an annual show. The Society celebrated its Diamond Jubilee in 2003.

Founder Chairman
Tom Kingsley

Cottered's branch of the Women's Institute was formed in 1942 and was active for over thirty years until it closed in 1984. At one time it had its own choir conducted by the headmaster of Cottered School, Lionel Howard. Like the Horticultural Society, the W. I. was involved in the founding of the village hall and in raising funds for it. Their Silver anniversary was held in November 1967.

Diana and Louise Sylvester at the Horticultural Show 1960

Members of the W.I. stage a fashion show 1959
L to r: Ann Davis, Verena Dale, Irene Edwards, Barbara Sharp,
Lilla Hearn, Joyce Cartwright, Molly Wilds and Audrey Silsby.

A Youth Club was begun by the Women's Institute in 1944, but dwindled and closed. It was re-established by the early 1960's.

Radio Disc Jockey Keith Fordyce with
members of the Youth Club 1963

The Cottered Banger Club, founded in 1968, took all the honours at the Brafield Stadium in Northamptonshire and was even featured on television's 'Blue Peter' programme. In 1972 it was replaced by the Cottered Short Circuit Club, which raced at Lower Farm, Throcking.

Cottered Short Circuit Club Ladies l. to r. Brenda Thorp, Ann Taylor, Helen Ashcroft, Barbara Claydon and Irene Murchie 1972
Photo Royston Crow

Grass track racing at Throcking 1972
Photo Royston Crow

The Cottered branch of the Royal British Legion was formed in 1947. The Branch was presented with its first Standard by William Sanders and dedicated on 16 November that year. In 1959 the Standard was paraded at the Service of Remembrance at the Royal Albert Hall and again in November 1980. Over the years, the Branch has raised much money for the Earl Haig Poppy Appeal through events such as an annual car boot sale, jumble sales, cheese and wine evenings.

In 1960 the Legion raised funds and erected a War Memorial Tablet in Cottered Church. A new Standard was presented by Peter Sanders, son of William Sanders, in 1975 and the old Standard was laid up.

*British Legion members march to
Cottered Church 1958*

*Brownies, Guides and members of
The British Legion parade 1972*

The 1st Cottered Brownies was formed in the late 1940's, disbanded and re-formed in 1968, lapsed and re-started in 2004. The 1st Cottered Guides were formed in 1948 but finally disbanded in 1977.

In 1978 the Friends of Cottered Church was founded through the efforts of Dick Edwards, then a Churchwarden and the group continues to raise much-needed funds for the repair and maintenance of the parish church. These fund-raising occasions have over the years become major social events in the village.

Dick Edwards

With the superb facilities at the new Village Hall, several new organisations have been formed. These include the Cottered Badminton Club and Carpet Bowls. A Lunch Club was also formed in 2002 and organises bi-monthly lunches cooked and served by local volunteers.

The Cottered Ramblers was formed at the beginning of 2004 and has become a popular monthly outdoor pursuit.

Cottered Ramblers on a walk 2004

Japanese Gardens

Herbert and Constance Goode in their Benz car 1900's
Photo loaned by Rose McKay

Constance Goode

The famous Japanese Gardens are hidden from the passer-by. They were first laid out by a wealthy china merchant, Herbert Goode, at the beginning of the 20th century, after he and his wife Constance had visited Japan.

At the turn of the 19th/20th century Japanese things became fashionable and Japanese gardens were created in Britain, such as those at Tatton Park, Powercourt and Compton Acres.

Mr Goode's interest grew and he acquired a practical knowledge of the Japanese style of gardening. He is said to have personally directed his men in placing the stone lanterns and images. In 1923 he obtained the services of Seyomon Kusumoto who built the two storied house, resting houses and other items to improve the idyllic setting. Seyomon, who lived in Cottered for a while, married a local girl.

The Sacred Bridge was built in Japan by Mr S Enemoto, modelled on the lines of the sacred bridge at Nikko. A Japanese Tea House built of many different types of wood was shipped over from Japan in 1912, as were many of the stone lanterns, rocks and colourful shrubs. In the mid 1920's, Herbert and Constance Goode moved into Cheynes House, which they had built. The Estate ensured jobs for local people at a period when there was high unemployment.

The Tea House, Japanese Gardens 2003

When Constance died in 1963, the estate was sold for £24,000 to the chairman of the Tetley tea firm, Tetley Tetley-Jones who at the time lived at Cottered Lordship.

During his period of ownership, a Canadian style Garden House was built in the Gardens and a number of alterations and improvements were made. A new Japanese style bridge replaced the wooden Evening View Bridge and some of the ornaments were re-sited. The two-storied Japanese house was enlarged and made into a guesthouse.

The Gardens were purchased by German couple Friedel and Elka Engelmann in 1971 but were sold by them in June 1985 to Graeme Woodhatch and his wife Susan who moved into

Garden House. In 1991 many items from the Gardens, including the wooden Fox Shrine, were spotted in a Sotheby's sale catalogue. It transpired that Graeme Woodhatch had tried to dispose of the listed and protected statuary. A roofing contractor, Woodhatch came to a grisly end when he was murdered by a Maori hit-woman in 1992.

New owners Ian and Carole Payne restored the missing Torri arches, wooden bridges and granite lanterns. They worked hard to restore the gardens to their former glory, putting the broken ornaments back together. In 1998 they sold the Japanese Gardens to the present owners and the gardens remain in private ownership.

The Fox Shrine 1934
Photo loaned by Duncan Saunders

Japanese Gardens in the snow 1963

Herbert Goode in his horse drawn carriage 1930's
Photo loaned by Rose McKay

Seyomon Kusomoto and his daughter re-visit the Japanese Gardens 1962

Ian and Carole Payne repair the broken stone ornaments on their return to Cottered 1997

The Weather

The area seems to escape most of the worst weather of England, but being on high ground is prone to heavy falls of snow often with high winds causing drifting.

Snow during Christmas 1927 was the worst since 1886. Winds exceeding 50 mph caused drifting along the Buntingford Road. At Tire Hill drifts ranged from four to eight feet. In March 1946 three cars were found in snowdrifts on the Cottered Road. Although roadmen and soldiers worked hard to cut a way through, the road was blocked for three days.

Arctic conditions hit the area in February 1947. Neville Chuck recalls, "Along with other school children, I joined the 'snow heaving' Gang, as they were known. But then it was found we were too young to get paid, so, rather disappointed, we didn't go back to work after the lunch break. However, I think some of the workmen had a whip round and gave us each a few shillings.

"When the thaw set in, there was flooding in the area. I remember that my father couldn't get home from work at Walkern because the water was rushing over the top of the metal railings of the bridge at Cromer."

February 1958 saw the worst blizzard for 30 years. The Cottered Road was completely blocked by snowdrifts for a couple of days. No fewer than 67 men dug along the Cottered to Buntingford Road in an effort to reach Buntingford. Many vehicles were stuck in the drifts.

The last day of 1961 saw roads blocked and villages isolated when fourteen inches of snow fell with drifts up to nearly three feet deep. The baker from Walkern reached the village in a Land Rover. No newspapers, or milk could be delivered and it was a couple of days before the mail could get through. Forty men who were unable to travel to work, dug about one and a half miles along the Buntingford Road before a bulldozer came to the rescue.

Lorries stuck on Lodge Hill, Baldock Road February 1958

Bert Cartwright and other workmen dig the road out at Brook End 1963

Residents at Cottered and Throcking had to contend with no mains water supply as well as a power cut caused by the snow in January 1963. Milk froze in the bottles as temperatures dropped to around -15 deg C. At Oxford the River Thames froze over.

Frozen milk 1963

The worst snowstorm for 20 years brought the locality to a standstill in February 1979. The strong northeasterly winds scoured exposed fields clean and the roads were filled to a depth of eight feet in many places. In response to the District Council's appeal for help in clearing the roads, the 'Cottered Conga Line,' was born. It consisted of caterpillar tracked vehicles driven by three local men, Alan Silver, David Pettitt and Malcolm Chapman. They worked for three days from 5 am to midnight in a bid to clear the Cottered to Buntingford road, but as fast as they cleared it the wind blew the snow back again.

Blizzards in December 1981 led to cars being abandoned. Cottered was cut off for at least 48 hours before the roads were cleared. Temperatures dropped to around -12 deg C! Six inches of snow fell during the night during February 1991; few people made it to work or school. A further four inches fell five days later.

Although only four inches of snow fell during one afternoon at the end of January 2003, many people left work early, but didn't get far as they found the roads were already blocked by abandoned vehicles. Many villagers didn't get home that night. The situation worsened when an articulated lorry jack-knifed completely blocking the Cottered to Buntingford road for the next couple of days! Drivers stranded in the village spent the night at Cottered Village Hall.

Floods are quite rare, but in 1968 the Baldock Road was closed due to flooding. There was also extensive flooding at Buntingford when the River Rib overflowed causing damage to houses in Vicarage Road, the High Street and at Corney Bury Farm.

Flood at the bottom of Lodge Hill, Baldock Road 1968

In August 1958 a freak whirlwind took some of the slates off the former Chapel. It also took the top out of a tree on Bowling Green and the washing off a line at the Village Shop, with Jim and Margaret Edwards' clothes ending up strewn across the Playing Field over 400 yards away!

Strong winds in March 1986 demolished a large barn at the former Rectory. The October 1987 gales caused damage to trees, and high winds in January 1990 damaged the roof of Southfield Farm just over the edge of the parish boundary.

The barn at the Old Rectory, March 1986

Finale

In conclusion, the community of Cottered is no longer as self-sufficient as it once was. People now have to travel to neighbouring towns, or further afield, both for employment and for most everyday requirements. A few villagers still grow much of their own produce, but they, like the rest of us, also rely on local supermarkets.

Over the last century, the proportion of people working within the parish has declined significantly. The need for agricultural labourers and stockmen has virtually disappeared and the village now has a higher proportion of residents in professional occupations.

There are now more houses than there used to be, but the population has not risen proportionately as families have become smaller. At one time, only a few residents owned their own houses. The smaller properties in the village were almost all rented. Now even much of the Local Authority housing, built for renting, has been sold and is owner-occupied.

The parish churches remain a stable and important part of village life. Attitudes have changed; people no longer fear losing their jobs if they fail to attend church, but the ministry of the church is still there to meet present day needs.

Although the community is not as close-knit as it once was, community spirit is still evident in the various activities and organizations.

As for the future, who knows? Young couples will, inevitably, be forced to leave the village for cheaper accommodation as house prices continue to soar. To survive, any community has to be able to embrace some changes and look forward to what lies ahead.

Note:
1 acre = $4,046.9m^2$

Index

Illustrations in *italics*